CLARIFYING WHAT MATTERS

CLARIFYING WHAT MATTERS

Creating Direction for Your Career

ERICA MATTISON

TABLE OF CONTENTS

CHAPTER 1:
WELCOME

This book is for you if you are ready to explore how to make positive changes in your life.

Are you feeling frustrated in your career and looking to upgrade to meaningful work that reflects your interests, digs deep into your experience and skillset, and incorporates challenges that excite you? I get it. I've been there, and so have my coaching clients. Through telling their stories and some of my own, my goal is to show you that you're not alone, that there's nothing (and I mean nothing!) inherently wrong with you if you haven't figured it out yet or are currently stuck, and that a more satisfying career path is waiting for you.

We've all faced uncomfortable obstacles at various points in our career journeys. In your case, maybe you've stayed at the same organization for several years despite a long-held desire to move on.

Perhaps you're part of an underrepresented group within your industry, and navigating issues regarding race, age, or sexual orientation in your workplace.

You may be the first in your family to complete a college degree or find yourself in an environment very different from your country and culture of origin.

If you've been bullied by a supervisor who didn't appreciate your value or treat you with respect, you might view certain industries as tainted because of that experience and cut yourself off from opportunities that could fulfill your goals.

Health challenges may have derailed you, making it difficult to focus on building a rewarding career.

Maybe you have a learning disability or ADHD, and have had a difficult time figuring out what types of settings help you flourish.

You may have struggled to establish healthy boundaries.

Or perhaps you've lost your job and have questioned your skills and value.

My experience as a certified career coach and master certified life coach has underscored how deeply and widely our personal lives and our professional lives affect one another. When your career is unbalanced, unsatisfying, or corrosive, your health, sleep, confidence, finances, and relationships suffer. So too do personal challenges have the ability to impact your professional life.

Career transitions are a natural part of life, and you will likely experience several throughout your life. My big picture goal is to help you feel hopeful that you can clarify what's important to you and move forward with a sense of direction. Through my coaching, people make changes with more ease. We hire experts for all sorts of areas of life— why not our careers?

Speaking to the rarely static nature of contemporary occupational journeys, my colleague Mark Franklin, a co-founder of OneLife-Tools, developed this definition of "career" as an invitation to shift your perspective.

CAREER: "Your career is the full expression of who you are and how you want to be in the world. And, it keeps on expanding as it naturally goes through cycles of stability and change."

Guiding Questions:

What does this definition of "career" bring up for you?

How might this perspective on careers influence your approach to your career?

CHAPTER 2:
MY CAREER JOURNEY

I acknowledge the role that privilege has played in my life. Knowing I had people who were there for me made a big difference in what I felt I was able to do. What people and organizations can you count on to support you during a period of career transition? Gratitude is a powerful companion to keep close as you step outside your comfort zone.

I've pretty much always marched to my own beat, writing my own job description on more than one occasion, moving cross-country to lead an organization whose mission I believed in, and leaving a good job to go all in with my coaching business. I recognize that privilege enabled me to attend a good public school, get an undergraduate degree, land several internships during and after college, build a robust network, and take risks.

Each of these actions was a way for me to fully express who I am. They increased my career and life satisfaction, a result of leaning into curiosity and my desire to make a positive impact on issues I care about. In every new situation, I learned new skills, expanded my network, grew my self-awareness, and was able to positively influence others to reach their own goals.

I was the first person to serve in a sustainability role at Suffolk University, and people regularly sought me out for vocational guidance. I earned a reputation as a career resource, particularly for those interested in the burgeoning field of sustainability. By mentoring people who were seeking to do work that makes a positive impact on society, I found I was able to combine my interests in personal growth, career development, psychology, and social impact.

As demand for my services grew, I decided to start a side business guiding people through career transitions. As I worked with clients, I derived great satisfaction from supporting them to build rewarding, mission-driven careers.

One of the first actions I took was reaching out to a career professional I knew. No need to reinvent the wheel about how to further my development as a coach. Michele and I were colleagues at Suffolk University, where we collaborated to create a guide on careers in sustainability. She recommended that I join the Career Counselors' Consortium Northeast, a group of career professionals in my area. I immediately became a member and started participating in their trainings. This helped me expand my network in the career and professional development world, which was key for learning more about industry leaders and best practices.

Eager to speed up my learning and provide the best career services possible, I invested in my professional development by participating in several training programs. Over the course of a few years, I reinvested revenue by obtaining certifications through the National Career Development Association and the Certified Life Coach Institute.

In addition, once I finished my Masters in Public Administration and my Juris Doctor at night while working at Suffolk University during the day, I had more capacity to lean into coaching.

What cemented the foundation of my coaching was participating in an in-depth self-leadership training program rooted in axiology, the science of ethics. My Uncle Marvin's longtime study and application of ethics inspired me to make that investment. By learning the best practices for helping people get out of their own way and tap into their most effective ways of being, I felt better equipped to serve clients.

Soon after, I became a certified coach with SkillScan, a career assessment tool which helps people focus, discover, explore, and market themselves. I went on to obtain a Holistic Narrative Career Professional (HNCP) Certification through OneLifeTools, which upleveled my skills in story-listening to help clients reflect on their experiences, and increase their clarity and proactivity.

Originally I did not consider leaving my career as an environmental professional to run my own coaching business. As a participant in SCORE, a business mentorship program sponsored by the US Small Business Administration, my mentor asked, "How are you going to grow your business when you have a full-time job?" The discomfort caused by this question caught my attention. As I reflected, I realized that my unsettled feeling pointed to a deep desire to join the many people in my network who were already self-employed.

Witnessing the transformative results of my work with clients motivated me to help even more people get unstuck. I needed enough time to work with clients one-on-one, lead trainings, write, and immerse myself in personal growth and career development. Leaving my 9-to-5 role as the director of strategic communications was something I started to seriously consider. "What would it be like to be able to focus more time and energy on my coaching practice?" I wondered. This was during the early days of the COVID pandemic, when many of my clients were rethinking their lives, and I decided to do the same.

Still undecided, I nevertheless took measures to prepare so that if I did decide to leave my job, I would be ready. I began to take steps to run my business in a more formal way – filing as an LLC, opening a business bank account, getting a bookkeeping system established, and the like. But perhaps most importantly, I worked on my mindset. After working as an employee for 20+ years, I needed to shift how I thought of myself and my career so I could prepare for the challenge of being self-employed and producing my income fully from my business.

And yet, some influential people in my life encouraged me to stay in the climate change space. They advised me to keep my steady paycheck and robust benefits package. They cautioned me about going out on my own. After all, I had built a reputation over years of creating and advancing sustainability programs and shaping statewide environ-mental policies. Whether intentional or not, their encouragement felt like unwelcome pressure. They eventually got on board with my shift to self-employment, but their concern for me and their belief in the im-portance of the work I was doing prevented them from doing so earlier.

While my passion for addressing climate change had not disap-peared, deep down, I knew it was time to shift my focus from working in communications to helping individuals fulfill their potential. Over time, my work with hundreds of clients and my own self-discovery process called me to lean into coaching full-time. I didn't want to regret not going for it. I didn't want to let fear hold me back and prevent me from allowing myself to trust my ability to figure it out.

At first, I mainly coached folks who shared my longstanding commitment to supporting vibrant communities, combining my experience and expertise in mission-driven areas like environmental protection, sustainability, climate action, clean energy, sustainable transportation, ESG (Environmental Social Governance), corporate citizenship, health equity, and environmental justice.

As the seasons transitioned, I prepared to transition out of my role as an employee and into my new role as a full-time self-employed entrepreneur. I delved into books, podcasts, articles, and workshops on entrepreneurship, small business management, and marketing. I set up conversations with several people who had already done what I was looking to do and learned their stories and best practices.

Now I was my own supervisor, experiencing the joys and challenges of life as a full-time entrepreneur. Instead of squeezing my business into early mornings, nights, and weekends, I was free to work on my business at any time of day, any day of the week.

Since going out on my own, I've derived great satisfaction from having more bandwidth to facilitate workshops, hone my approach to coaching, write about career development, and build lasting relationships with fellow coaches, entrepreneurs, and clients. Had I not made the leap, I would have always wondered, "What if?"

Guiding Questions:

Have you ever felt pressured to choose or maintain a specific trajectory? If so, you're not alone.

CHAPTER 3:
HOW TO TRANSFORM
YOUR CAREER

I have extensive direct experience with career transitions.

I've gone from Concierge Service Professional in the hospitality industry as a new graduate, to Campaign Field Organizer for John Kerry for President, to Legislative Aide in state government, to Executive Director of a women's legislative organization. From there, I leaned into my longstanding passion for environmental issues, working at my graduate school as the first Recycling Coordinator and then first Sustainability Coordinator. Throughout my upbringing, my parents' involvement on the local level provided me with a context for thinking about environmental policy issues.

Once I completed my law degree as an evening student, I was excited to combine my environmental and public policy experience as Legislative Director at a leading statewide environmental protection advocacy organization. After a few years as a lobbyist, I chose to challenge myself by moving cross-country to serve as Executive Director of a grassroots nonprofit that uses a community-based model to increase access to greenspace and improve climate resiliency.

I realized that I wanted to have a narrower role that was focused on my strengths in areas like relationship building, strategy development, and communications. So, I moved into a communications-oriented role within a university sustainability office. I started as Assistant Director and successfully advocated for a promotion to Director of Strategic Communications.

This career journey included a variety of roles, industries, and sectors. Some of the roles and organizations were better fits than others for me. But every time I landed one of these roles, I was excited and saw a lot of potential to join others creating more sustainable communities.

For years, I worked as a freelance coach and consultant in addition to my 9-to-5 roles.

After I transitioned to full-time coach, I took everything I learned from these experiences and applied it to growing my business, serving clients as a champion and advisor.

What Made All of These Transitions Possible?

Through hiring my own coaches to support and guide me, I've learned to reflect on my career and clarify strengths and patterns that have enabled me to move forward with intentionality.

Throughout my career, I have tapped into my existing strengths while building skills and growing my network. Developing an empowered, proactive approach to my career is something I have prioritized and now help my clients achieve.

What I've come to understand is that my career transitions were possible because I believed in myself. Not that it was always easy, but I knew that I could learn new skills and take on roles I'd never served in before. I believed that I could bounce back from challenging situations. I have cultivated a growth mindset that helps me see new situations as learning opportunities.

Having a growth mindset as an adult is not innate, but learned, honed with each new stage of expansion.

Having a growth mindset as an adult is not innate, but learned, honed with each new stage of expansion. It's a constant process that I'm continuously engaged in personally and with others, and this familiarity allows me to teach the practices that work best at any stage.

How Were These Transitions Beneficial?

Each new organization and role I served in enabled me to begin again.

I was able to apply lessons learned from one situation to another. For instance, earlier in my career, when I would start in a new role, I would immediately set about finding problems and identifying ways to improve systems. I love to innovate and some of my previous roles called for me to create new programs from scratch. But what I learned is that this approach can alienate colleagues who developed or maintained the current approaches. It took a few tough situations and several years to recognize that my approach needed some finesse. Perhaps if I had had the benefit of some coaching earlier in my career, I would have learned this lesson sooner!

Eventually, I learned that trusting relationships are crucial building blocks for creating change, and that people want to feel acknowledged and recognized. This seems obvious, but my desire to use my creativity to make positive changes often got in the way of focusing on relationship-building. To be an effective agent for change, it's necessary to build strong relationships and put people over systems.

A few years ago, when a hiring supervisor asked me in a job interview how I would transform the organization's communications, my response was informed by the missteps I had made in the past. I shared that I would first seek to understand how the current communications practices had come into being and evolved, and then I would consult with various key stakeholders to identify needs and opportunities to inform changes. I got the job.

Guiding Questions

Reflecting on a challenge you faced, what are your insights about your ability to overcome hurdles?

How can your personal qualities and strengths help you when you encounter future challenges? (An example of a personal quality is curiosity. An example of a strength is problem solving.)

CHAPTER 4:
SUPPORTING CLIENTS THROUGH THEIR CAREER CHANGE

Having learned to tap into my stories to identify opportunities for my own career, I am able to guide my clients to use their stories to reflect on past experiences, clarify what they want and don't want in their work lives, and redirect towards a more rewarding career.

It's common to think that you don't have the necessary credentials or experience for your desired work and to be concerned that becoming qualified is out of reach. Another common concern is that what you want isn't feasible. For instance, it may seem like it's not realistic to switch industries without starting over in an entry-level role. Or maybe what you want to do seems like it's not something that can earn you a good living. And so, we stay in our current situation out of fear that what we want won't work out.

Storytelling helps me guide my clients to more nimbly adapt. For instance, when seeking to make a career pivot from one industry or issue area to another, it's necessary to speak the language of your target audience. A move from a for-profit company to a nonprofit organization calls for language to shift from "customers" to "members, supporters, and partners."

Often, we are so consumed with the busyness of daily tasks that we fail to focus a sufficient amount of our resources on what's truly important to us. If it's valuable to you to lead a rewarding, impactful career, it's crucial that you discover what—and who—is going to help you do that.

Expanding Your Perspective Through Feedback

In addition to sharing their own perspective, I encourage clients to seek feedback from trusted allies. These could be friends, family, mentors, or colleagues they have strong relationships with. Specific, meaningful feedback can be hard to come by. I constantly hear from people that they are hungry for helpful feedback but don't know how to get it.

By inviting others' perspectives on our qualities and possibilities, there is a lot we can learn. In addition, the ability to graciously receive feedback is a worthwhile skill to develop. I guide my clients through how to collect feedback and incorporate the most meaningful aspects into their vision for their future. This process also helps them realize they're not alone and that they have support – valuable realizations for creating a rewarding career.

Re-engaging With Your Network

Making a number of pivots in my career and working as an environmental protection lobbyist has helped me learn the importance relationships play in creating a fulfilling career. To make it easier for people to give you a chance and listen to you, it helps for them to know you, trust you, like you, and to understand how you create value (aka how you can help them advance their goals).

It's easy to become so busy that we forget to keep in touch with our network. I can't tell you the number of clients I've worked with who have said to me something along the lines of, "I don't know how to ask people I know for help with my career because it's been so long since I've talked to most of them."

Sound familiar?

Fortunately, these concerns can be addressed. Over the years, working with hundreds of clients, I have honed my system for activating networks. It goes like this:

- Inventory your network

- Analyze your network

- Re-engage with your network

- Identify opportunities to grow your network

- Prioritize your outreach

- Develop a practice of engaging with your network

Make engagement with your network part of your daily life – not just something you do when you want something from people.

Note how authenticity and service are the foundation here. Within a matter of weeks, clients who previously felt unsure of how to reach out to people in their circles who could help them—and maybe even dreaded it—gain more comfort and confidence. They revitalize their networks, expand their connections, and have fun doing it.

It's common for people to lack awareness of just how extensive their networks are. I help my clients by identifying existing connections and nurturing the relationships they'd like to strengthen, for instance with colleagues—past and present, friends, and community members. And again, because it cannot be overstated, the focus is on mutual bene-fit, rather than begging for favors. The shift of perception that highlights both parties offering and receiving reduces the stress people often asso-ciate with the phrase "networking." Instead, clients uncover professional opportunities while increasing their sense of connection.

Guiding Questions

What is a relationship that influenced your career trajectory?

How did your interaction with that person shape your career?

What lessons can you learn from this example?

CHAPTER 5: FACILITATING PURPOSEFUL CAREER TRANSITIONS

You've invested in yourself over the years, possibly earning degrees and certifications. You believe in continuous learning and improvement, professionally and personally, and you feel it's important to be part of an organization that shares this commitment. You want to be supported in your efforts to innovate.

However, when it comes to your professional life, you've experienced a high level of frustration and stress for a long time—months, years, possibly even decades. You're not sure what to do about it. You feel stuck and fearful of continuing to repeat that which isn't working for you. The anxiety that you're feeling about your career is affecting your health, sleep, energy, finances, and social life, as well as the activities you once enjoyed.

On the macro level, you want to contribute to an organization that is moving issues forward—ones that you care about, like climate change and racial and gender equity. Maybe you're involved in some local efforts, like your community's sustainability committee or a faith organization working on social justice issues.

You're creative. You love solving problems and working collaboratively. You have skills in areas like communication and leadership; deep down, you know that you have a lot to offer, but sometimes you could use a reminder about how capable you are.

If only you could figure out how to lead a more fulfilling career! What could become possible through your work? What would it mean for the other parts of your life as well?

Using Your Stories to Clarify What Matters to You

When you feel like there are a lot of options and you don't know which direction to go, it's natural to feel overwhelmed and like your thoughts are a big, jumbled ball of yarn.

It might surprise you to learn that storytelling is a powerful tool for unraveling that tangle of overwhelm. I support my clients to increase their clarity by helping them tap into their lived experiences. From there, I use interactive ideation and tracking tools to help clients clarify their desired career. From a foundation of clarity, they can more naturally take inspired action, which, in turn, builds momentum. By learning to proactively steward their career – not just react in times of turmoil – the clients I serve develop consistency. This is crucial for building momentum, which is extremely important for creating positive change. Without a feeling of momentum, things languish, creating a feeling of being stuck.

Through coaching, I help clients reflect and clarify so they can become unstuck. "Our sessions really help me organize my thoughts," a client shared with me.

As a complement to SkillScan, I introduce my clients to a highly structured, fun, and visual narrative assessment model. I first learned about using storytelling to propel folks forward onto a satisfying career path while presenting at the Global Annual Conference of the National Career Development Association (NCDA) in Chicago. I met some fellow presenters, and they shared their evidence-based, gamified framework for tapping into the power of people's stories. I was immediately intrigued. I trained in their narrative assessment methodology and integrated it into my coaching practice. As I served dozens of clients in the subsequent months, I honed my story-listening skills and became adept at helping clients clarify who they are, what's important to them, and what possibilities they're curious to explore.

"The storytelling approach has been a confidence booster, helping me recognize and leverage my skills. Reflecting on past experiences has allowed me to identify areas for growth and strategic skill development." - Julie Nguyen, Client

Guided storytelling helps people realize that even their negative experiences present learning opportunities. For instance, by helping someone say what they don't want, we can identify what they do want for the future. A client of mine, Alex, was at his best when he was in collaborative settings, but his work felt isolating. Guided storytelling helped him identify that a social, team-oriented environment and role were must-haves. With this awareness, Alex was able to clarify what he wanted, seek out team-centered opportunities, and be proactive about building relationships at work and beyond.

Moving from Clarity to Exploration

I regularly hear people say, "I need a plan for my career/job search/career pivot." This desire to feel organized and intentional is understandable, because creating a plan can build a sense of empowerment and a feeling that you're strategically focusing your time and energy.

Once I support clients to reflect on their experiences and increase their level of clarity, I help them shift to intentional exploration. Within the OneLifeTools online storytelling platform, I support my clients in developing Exploration Plans so they can accelerate and track tangible progress toward their goals. After identifying clues, it's time to focus on taking inspired actions such as conducting online searches, reading books and articles, volunteering, and having intentional conversations.

Guiding Questions

When was the last time you identified your top skills and their importance to you?

How could increasing your awareness of these skills impact your quality of life?

How would having a thought partner to help clarify and articulate your strengths make a difference for you?

CHAPTER 6:
FROM UNSURE TO EXCITED
IN UNDER A MONTH

Humans have been telling stories for ages. Since our cave days, stories have served as templates, inspiration, and instruction. Stories help us build bridges to other people, feel connected, learn about ourselves and the world, and discover who we want to be around.

The following are real examples of people just like you who were able to move into roles more aligned with their personal interests and goals.

Sometimes, your dream job comes to you in an unexpected way.

When Victoria came to me, she was feeling deeply discouraged. After leaving a company where she'd worked for a dozen years, she was exhausted and unsure about what type of organization would be a good match for her next career phase. After weathering some unpleasant instances of dysfunction in her organization, she was eager to be part of a high-functioning, supportive team where she could apply her skills and feel valued, while increasing her sense of financial stability.

After our introductory session, Victoria began diligently working on the agreed-upon assignments. We were scheduled to meet at the end of the week, but before then I received this email from her:

"I have some good news. I interviewed with a local organization today for a temporary part-time position, and our conversation went so well that the director invited me to have a follow-up conversation with him and his colleague next week to discuss a possible full-time salaried position, which would be my dream job!"

The type of role Victoria went on to describe is exactly what I imagined for her, based on what she shared with me about her desires and strengths just a couple of weeks ago during our coaching session.

I offered to move up our session to the beginning of the week so I could help her prepare. To help Victoria focus her time and energy efficiently and effectively, I provided her with my Interview & Negotiation Preparation Guides, which I have developed and refined over the years.

Less than a month into our work together, she was already being considered for exciting professional opportunities aligned with her interests and goals.

From Stuck to Energized

When John S. came to me, he had been working at the same organization for over a decade and was completely depleted. We had connected earlier in our careers through our work in the environmental space, and had kept in touch.

For years, he had considered furthering his education but wasn't sure what he would want to study or how he would pay for it. He was feeling conflicted—on the one hand, he was feeling stagnant in his career, but on the other hand, he was feeling grateful to have a good job with an organization doing mission-driven work.

He wanted to make a change in his career to feel more challenged but wasn't sure exactly what he wanted to do or how to market himself. He also wanted to match his current level of compensation, or even increase it, without sacrificing his values.

Through our work together, we identified what was standing in his way. As he raised his self-awareness, he built his confidence and engaged more proactively with his network. He started to discover opportunities he was excited about and began to feel less fearful about the possibility of leaving his longtime employer for something new and different.

As we continued together, he gained comfort sharing his story and advocating for himself to create win-win situations, which enabled him to successfully navigate the interview and negotiation processes, which resulted in an offer with a 25% pay increase. His new role in a different industry enables him to feel expansive instead of stuck. On top of that, thanks to a great benefits package that includes tuition remission, he's finally able to take the graduate school courses he's been dreaming of for years.

Once John made the decision to work with a coach and welcome the possibility of change, within a few months he was able to secure a terrific role that enabled him to learn and grow, and feel more fulfilled and satisfied in his work life, creating positive effects in his personal life as well.

Overcoming his fears made it possible to have a high level of career satisfaction—he's contributing to a cause he cares about, expanding his skillset, and has the flexibility he needs as a parent. Not only that, but the financial stability this creates for his family is enabling his spouse the freedom to pursue her entrepreneurial vision.

One night, several months into his new role, I connected with John and a few of his colleagues at an event. It was truly gratifying to hear them rave about how thrilled they are to have him as a co-worker.

From Frustrated to Elated in Under Two Months

After struggling for two years on her own, my client Polly M. was able to secure a new job within two months, thanks to our work together. She wanted to transition from independent consulting to full-time employment at a mission-driven organization that reflected her values. As a single parent, it was important to her to create financial stability for her family and have the flexibility to be an engaged parent.

Before Polly started working with me, she was landing interviews, but no job offers. She had made it to the final round of interviews for a few different positions. "What do I need to do differently?" she asked herself. Once I helped Polly pinpoint mindsets and actions that were holding her back from achieving her goals, I provided support to make some necessary shifts. An outside perspective from a coach who emboldens you can make a huge difference.

By increasing her self-awareness and building her confidence,

Polly discovered the best roles for her to apply for, as well as how to position herself effectively to land job offers.

Soon after, Polly secured a job offer and went on to flourish in a community and volunteer engagement role with the Massachusetts chapter of a leading nonprofit organization. Her work as a leader in her organization is stimulating and meaningful, and she's been able to build on her years of experience as a consultant. Her new role helped her create the financial stability and flexibility that are so important to her.

Guiding Questions

What's important to you?

Are you ready to receive support to clarify and welcome into your life what matters to you?

CHAPTER 7:
FROM STRESSED OUT TO
AT EASE IN ONE SEASON

Jill S. was struggling with the direction she wanted to go in for her career. She was looking for ways to learn, grow, and advance in her career, and it was important to her to contribute to a community-minded mission. However, she wasn't confident in her ability to make a pivot to another type of work, and she was having difficulty making decisions. In addition, she was interested in furthering her education but was unsure about what type of academic program would be a good fit.

Once she became a client, Jill had the support and structure to focus on her career development. She tapped into what drove her and learned to ease up and treat herself with more compassion.

Within weeks of starting our work together, Jill had better clarity and felt more confident and purposeful. She became more comfortable reaching out to people in her target industries, began to see herself as a leader, and identified an ideal graduate program. Most importantly, she felt more prepared to share her story, which helped her craft a compelling personal statement that was a big factor in her admission to the program.

She is thriving as a graduate student and continues to consider work opportunities that could be a good fit for her next chapter. She shared that the empowerment she developed through coaching has transformed her thought patterns and actions, improving her overall health and happiness. Her new demeanor has positively altered the daily quality of life for her and her family. Her husband commented to her how much more relaxed she is now.

These are just a few of my clients' success stories. Every month, I generate new ones, and I'm excited to share those with you in the future.

CHAPTER 8:
DREAM, PLAN, ACT

Realizing What You Have to Offer

It's common for people to dismiss or not realize what they have to offer, resulting in a limited view of what's possible. As a coach, it's important to remind people of their strengths and build comfort in communicating about them. Repeat after me: "Sharing about what I have to offer is not bragging." When you increase your self-awareness of your strengths, you are better equipped to identify and attract opportunities aligned with your interests. I'm able to help clients develop this awareness within a short period of time. They not only understand their strengths better, but how they can combine their strengths with their interests in new and exciting ways.

I often witness people minimizing what matters to them, thinking it's trivial or infeasible. I've especially noticed this among women I speak with, particularly when it comes to hobbies, passion projects, and volunteer work. The patriarchal worldview that shapes so much of our thoughts, feelings, and actions would have us believe that something isn't valuable if it's enjoyable, especially if it has yet to yield much revenue.

Sharing about what I have to offer is not bragging.

To move past these barriers, I help my clients recognize and embrace what they enjoy, who they want to be, and how they wish to serve society. It's important not to let concerns about "how" get in the way of imagining the "why," the "what," and the "who." I support folks to deftly get out of their own way and give themselves permission to break free from their self-judgment and concerns about what others might think. The safe space we create together allows for dreaming and, from there, planning and taking action.

Through coaching, we address mindset barriers so that you can start taking tangible steps to create the kind of future you've so far only dreamt about. Systemic rubrics enable us to track information and reveal patterns which yield insights. For instance, creating a data hub for roles and organizations that interest you makes it possible to clarify what you want to focus on. From there, I help you determine concrete next steps.

Guiding Questions

What is a hobby or interest of yours that you diminish because it has not been a money-maker for you thus far or some might consider it "silly"?

How might the world benefit, even in some small way, from you embracing this interest and sharing it with more people?

CHAPTER 9:
THE SKILLS YOU WANT
TO APPLY

Do you struggle to identify your skills? How about determining the overlap of what you enjoy and what you're good at? What about the intersection of what you enjoy, what you're good at, and what you can earn a good living doing? If so, you're not alone.

In Japanese tradition, there is a concept called Ikigai. It blends two words: "iki" meaning "to live," and "gai" meaning "reason," which translates to "a reason to live." It is often represented by several concentric circles which represent areas such as what you love, what you're good at, what the world needs, and what you can be rewarded for. It is said that clarifying and cultivating a reason to live is key to living a fulfilling life.

This is not work that happens overnight, but you can achieve progress in much less time than you think, when you have the necessary motivation, support, and tools. If you've languished too long doing work misaligned with who you are and what's important to you, it can feel like an insurmountable challenge to figure out what you want, believe it's possible to achieve, and take the necessary steps to make it your reality. The longer you've been in an ill-fitting situation, the more of a challenge you can have in recognizing the possibilities that exist for you.

When switching from one kind of role or industry to another, it's crucial that you have a high level of self-awareness regarding your transferable skills. In other words, strategies, innovations, and capabilities developed in one type of setting can be applied to another. I have guided hundreds of clients through planning and executing career pivots and career advancement, and have developed a deep understanding of the best practices.

An important differentiation to make is between skills and

strengths. Think of your strengths as the skills you possess and want to use moving forward. In other words, your strengths are your skills that are most important to you. All too often, people just focus on what they're good at, but they forget about what they want to do. To create a truly satisfying work life, it's important to focus on the intersection of these areas, giving more attention to your strengths than simply your skills.

One of the tools I use to help clients clarify their strengths, opportunities for growth, and career possibilities is SkillScan. Through an online self-assessment and an in-depth, personalized report, I assist clients in identifying their top skill categories among management/leadership, communication, relationships, creative, physical/technical, and analytical. Within each category, I guide my clients to understand their top abilities, such as writing, brainstorming, researching, analyzing, building teams, serving clients and customers, and collaborating.

By understanding and clearly communicating what you have to offer, you can build your ability to target and attract opportunities that are a good match for you. My clients regularly say that coaching, along with the help of tools I connect them with, affirms distinct talents which boosts confidence. By becoming aware of specific themes and possibilities, they perceive their career more broadly, spotting opportunities that would have otherwise passed them by. And they're better equipped to present themselves for opportunities they're interested in, having a stronger sense of how to describe their relevant qualifications.

Momentum is a Motivator

As clients increase their sense of empowerment and develop a more proactive approach to their career and life choices, they spend less time and energy worrying and invest more resources in their learning and growth. A "virtuous cycle" is created. The momentum builds, and they're motivated to continue progressing.

As situations abound to meet people, engage with their networks, and participate in interesting conversations, they embrace curiosity and perceive their daily activities and interactions as learning opportunities. They often receive invitations to join boards, serve as consultants, teach courses, publish articles, and speak at conferences. More opportunities of interest come their way and scenarios that seemed impossible or improbable for a long time start coming to fruition.

Working together could be a valuable next step if you are eager for a fresh perspective to help you jump-start or sustain momentum. As a team, we will uncover experiences from your professional and personal life that hold clues for your future. I've found that mapping out these discoveries is a key ingredient in sparking momentum and helps clients "get unstuck"–moving past unsatisfying careers and unhelpful patterns into empowerment and fulfillment.

Guiding Questions

What's one project or initiative that you worked on at any point in your life that you found extremely rewarding? (Maybe it was paid work, or maybe it wasn't)

What made the experience interesting for you?

What are some skills you developed through the experience that you would like to use moving forward?

CHAPTER 10: THE IMPORTANCE OF REFLECTION

A core tenet of coaching is continuous reflection. Cultivating this as a practice is fundamental to self-awareness and growth. It's easy to say to yourself, "I'm going to reflect." But where to begin? It's transformative to have the support and structure that helps you actively and regularly engage in an awareness-raising practice.

If you're committed to continuous improvement for yourself and any organizations you want to help thrive, it's necessary to create the space and time to focus on your growth. By working with an experienced career practitioner, you can facilitate the process and enjoy a sense of flow.

As an outside party, I'm able to look at situations with fresh eyes. At the same time, I bring expertise from having worked with hundreds of individuals and organizations. This blend of freshness and familiarity enables me to support my clients to speed up their learning, growth, and progress.

One of my abilities is to help folks alternate between zooming in and out so they can focus on the details, while receiving relevant information from a big-picture view. This shifting of perspectives helps us notice patterns and opportunities. When we spend a high percentage of our time focused on minutiae, it's common to miss the big picture. But when we're overly focused on the big picture, we tend to miss crucial details that can help advance our vision.

For instance, my client Helen, a director who had just switched to a different tech company, came to me for executive coaching. She was feeling insecure in her new role leading a team of technical professionals, and it was important to her to get off to a strong start. During our first session, I helped her articulate some learning and growth goals. From there, I introduced her to a framework and tools to make headway on the specific milestones we established. Within a short timeframe, Helen reported considerable improvement in her ability to approach her leadership role with more confidence and effectiveness.

Guiding Questions

What is the top concern you have about your ability to be effective?

What becomes possible for you when you learn to step into your potential to serve as a confident, effective leader?

What becomes possible for your organization? Your community? The world?

CHAPTER 11:
KEEPING AN OPEN MIND

Sometimes, we disregard opportunities that could be a good fit for us.

Though it's surprising, given my long-standing passion for writing and public speaking, I was many years into my career before I had the word "Communications" in my job title. As a student, I had visions of continuing with my student journalism activities and becoming a professional journalist. It wasn't until I had honed communication skills through a number of roles and worked in some roles that were not a great fit, that I seriously considered a communications-focused opportunity.

The opportunity came at the right moment—I was looking to move from a generalist role as the executive director of a small nonprofit to a role that was more specialized. I wanted to continue working on issues that mattered to me, and environmental issues were something I've been passionate about since childhood. My parents, local environmental leaders, set an example of how to make a positive difference by organizing and advocating to create more healthy, sustainable communities. It's always been important to me to discover ways to serve as an environmental steward. And at this moment in my career, I was seeking to combine my passion for environmental issues with my strengths in a new way so I could continue to be challenged and find satisfaction in my work.

A relationship from my past opened a door. A sustainability colleague I had known years earlier was seeking someone with communications expertise to join his growing team at Boston University Sustainability. With the University's recently released Climate Action Plan in place and commitments by the University leadership to be bold on climate, there was a window of opportunity to have a powerful impact.

One of my consulting clients recommended I apply for the new sustainability communications role. I had previously seen the job posting, but had initially decided not to apply. It was not in my plans to return to campus sustainability work after seven years in that field earlier in my career. But after one or two people who knew me sent me the job posting, I decided not to close the door on the opportunity. By keeping an open mind, I realized that leading communications for the sustainability office at one of the largest research universities in the US would not be a step back in my career, but a coming together of different areas of expertise I had developed over the years.

It was this shift in mindset that enabled me to put myself forward as a candidate for the role. I notified the hiring manager, submitted my tailored job application, prepared for my job interview, and within weeks, I had secured a job offer.

My extensive network and reputation within the sustainability arena in Massachusetts played a key role in helping me land an interview. Being qualified for a role is important, but beyond that, when there is a lot of competition for an opportunity, it can be extremely helpful to have contacts familiar with you and your accomplishments. My past work in higher education sustainability had made it possible for me to encounter people in the field, including the person whose team I would join at Boston University (BU).

Working at BU gave me insight into how large organizations function and their broad reach of influence. Plus, serving as the project lead for the office's brand repositioning and new website development helped me build transferable skills that I would later tap into as an entrepreneur.

Guiding Questions

What is an existing relationship you'd like to revive?

What is a skill you're interested in tapping into for your future, even if it has yet to be part of your job title?

CHAPTER 12:
UNCOVERING NEW
DIRECTIONS

Through coaching you can discover new possibilities for directions in your professional and personal life.

For instance, my client Polly hadn't considered searching for "Engagement" on job boards, but through our work together, she realized that this phrase accurately represented a type of work she is well suited for. Once she made some adjustments to her search criteria, she was able to find a role that sounded like a great fit. Because she had the support to transform her job application materials and was able to tailor them for a particular opportunity, she immediately received an invitation to interview. Since we were already working together and could shift our focus to preparing for interviews, Polly was more confident and prepared to engage with the employer. Within a few weeks, she had landed and negotiated an offer she was excited to accept.

Our work is about clarifying who you are, what's important to you, and how to live authentically.

Through personalized coaching services, my clients and I co-create highly tailored experiences that meet them where they are and help them tap into their questions and experiences to identify and advance possibilities they're excited about. They have the support they need to expand their concept of what's possible, speed up their progress, and make decisions that are aligned with their values and priorities. They discover opportunities and contacts they weren't previously tuned in to, and learn how to take intentional actions that are sustainable. Our work together is about more than getting a new job or a promotion. Our work is about clarifying who you are, what's important to you, and how to live authentically.

Guiding Questions

What is one word or phrase you haven't been taking into consideration for your future that could help you identify new possibilities?

What is an idea for weaving together various threads from your past in a new and interesting way?

CHAPTER 13:
TOGETHER, WE CAN GO
SO MUCH FURTHER

I build bridges between people so they can feel supported and go further. I often think to myself, "Wouldn't it be wonderful if these people connected?"

Making introductions between people who have synergistic skills and interests flows from my desire to be of service. I typically make several introductions each week—online through platforms like LinkedIn and in person at events and spaces like my coworking community. Who knows where these new connections may lead? There are so many possibilities.

I connect hiring managers to prospective job candidates. I connect thought leaders who are working on the same public policy issues. I connect students with professionals in their target industries. I connect consultants with prospective clients.

"Erica is an incessant bridge builder. When Erica makes connections, new ideas sprout, and new possibilities are imaginable. I've been a personal beneficiary of Erica's bridge building countless times!" - Boston University Earth & Environment Professor and Climate Activist Dr. Nathan Phillips

Magic happens when the right people connect. One person has a skill, connection, experience, idea, resource, or quality another person needs to advance their goals and fulfill their potential. When these people come together, it's exciting.

Connections are mysterious. We don't know where they will lead, and that's OK. Relationship building isn't about knowing exactly where things will lead. It's about connecting, building trust, sharing, learning, growing, supporting, and collaborating. Relationships unfold over time.

I'm excited to connect with you and explore how I can support you on your journey.

Guiding Questions

Who are two people you know who you think could benefit from knowing each other?

Why do you think they could benefit?

When will you reach out to each of them to explore if there is mutual interest in an introduction?

CHAPTER 14:
GETTING STARTED WRITING
YOUR NEXT CHAPTER

Getting started can be the toughest part of any project, whether you're writing a book, launching a business, making a career pivot, or stepping into a leadership role.

Remember, you don't need to try to figure out everything on your own. I specialize in helping clients break down overwhelming projects into micro components to make them manageable. I guide people through a myriad of quandaries, such as determining their target salary range, how to leave their organization gracefully, their ideal start date for their new role—and how to advocate for it, how to identify their target market for their business, and how to become more confident leaders in their organizations.

To help them tap into the power of their networks, I often ask my clients, "Who do you know who might have some relevant knowledge here?" Building a robust support network is crucial to leading a rewarding career. Many people who come to me feel unsure about engaging with their networks and benefit from guided, intentional support.

I have successfully navigated these challenges myself and with many people. I welcome the opportunity of co-navigating with you to your dream career. Partnering with an experienced guide can help you make your journey less stressful and more enjoyable.

GRATITUDE

I'm grateful to my parents–Arlene and Hugh Mattison, my whole family, and Julio Cardenas for their support and guidance over the years. I'm grateful to the many mentors, supporters, and friends who have joined me on this journey, believing in me and encouraging me to live boldly.

Thank you to my Feedback Circle and editing team, who provided valuable insights for this book: Carol Adams, Jacklyn Janeksela, Jayne Young, Janice Nelson and Kim Douglas at Write to Unite, Jessica Cole at Bloomsday Literary, Laurel Clark, Lesah Beckhusen, and Nathan Phillips. Thank you to Hannah Abell for her proofreading work and Phuc Luu for the beautiful book design.

ABOUT THE AUTHOR

Erica Mattison, MPA, JD is an Executive Coach, a Certified Career Advisor, a Master Certified Life Coach, and CEO of Erica Mattison Coaching & Consulting.

From developing sustainability programs and communications strategies to serving as an environmental protection lobbyist and nonprofit board chair, Erica has a wealth of direct experience creating impact.

Erica has supported hundreds of social impact professionals to confidently navigate their careers. Through one-on-one coaching and group workshops, she helps purpose-driven professionals do good in the world and do well in their lives.

She is based in Boston, MA and works with clients near and far.

Erica enjoys dancing, bicycling, gardening, and connecting with people from all over the world.

Learn more and explore working together at ericamattison.com